MW01356645

This Book Belongs To

SMALL PREVIEW OF WHAT'S INSIDE

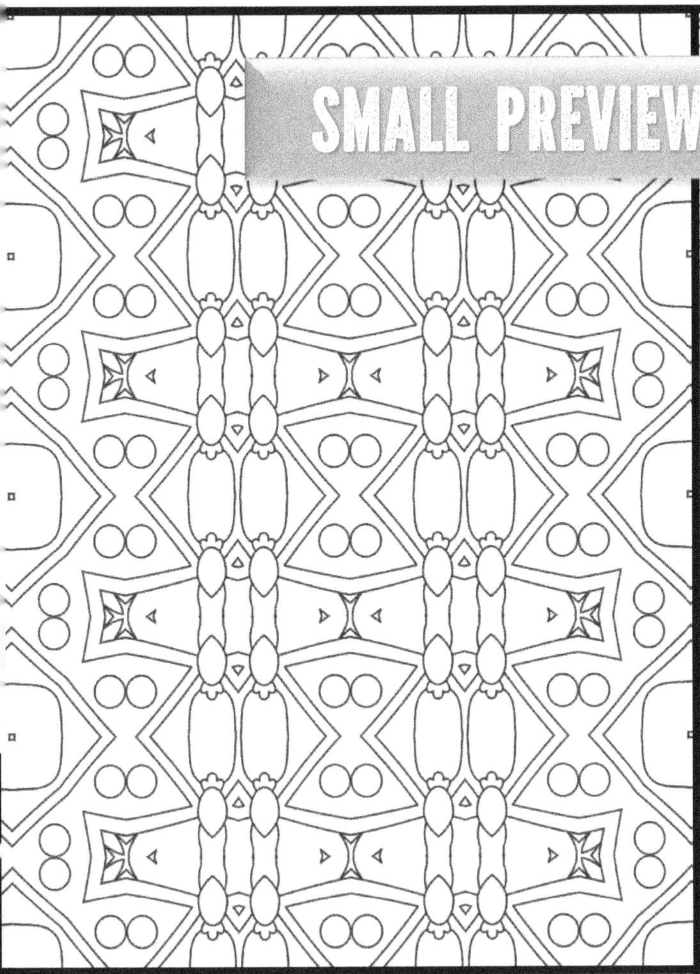

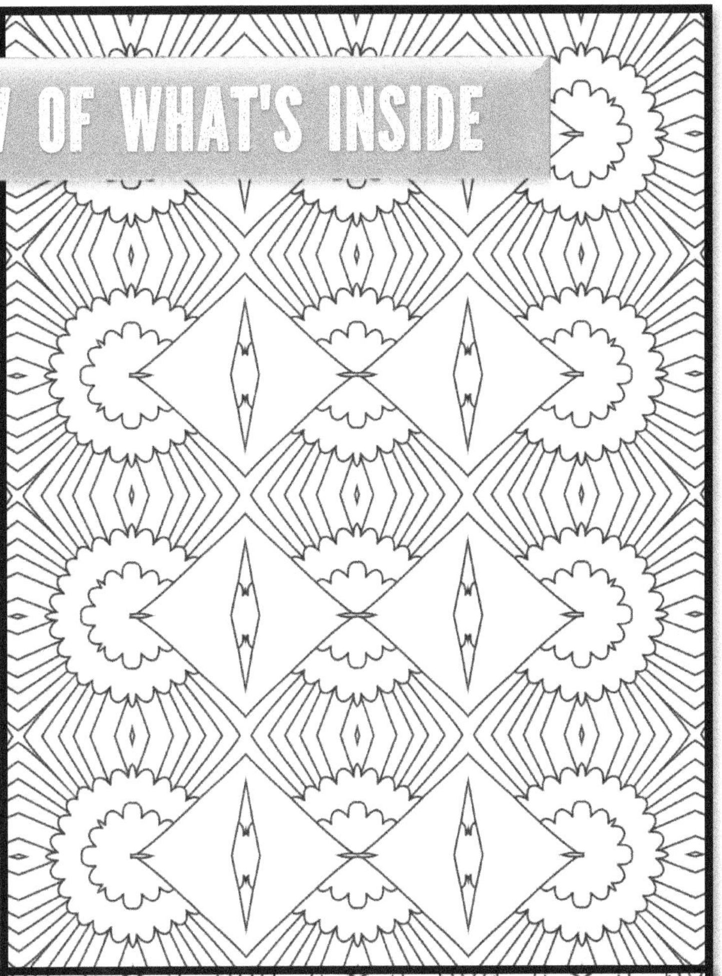

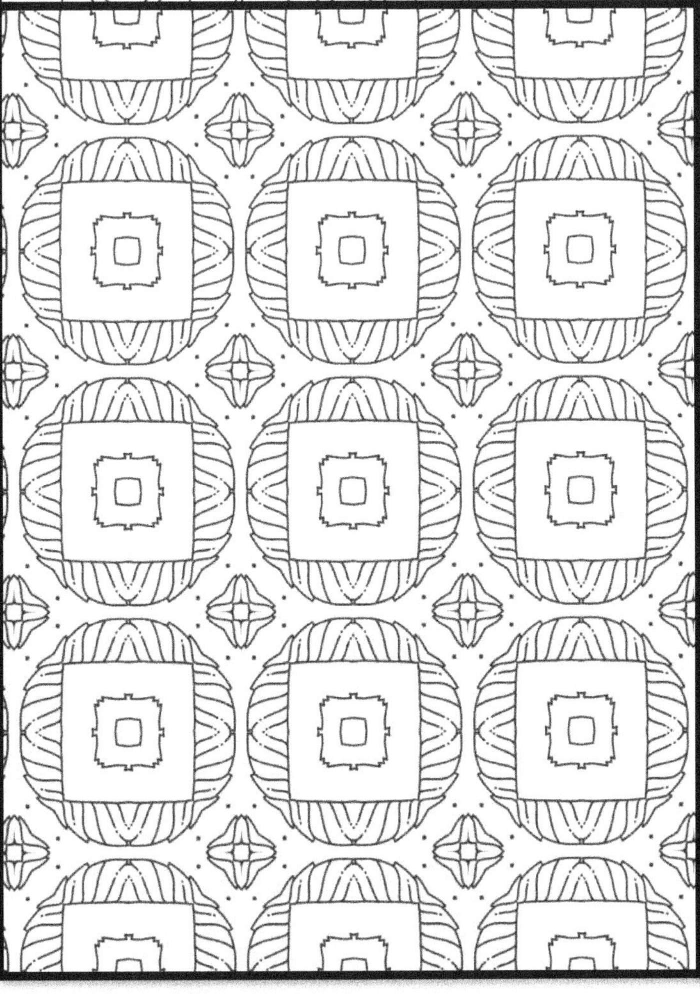

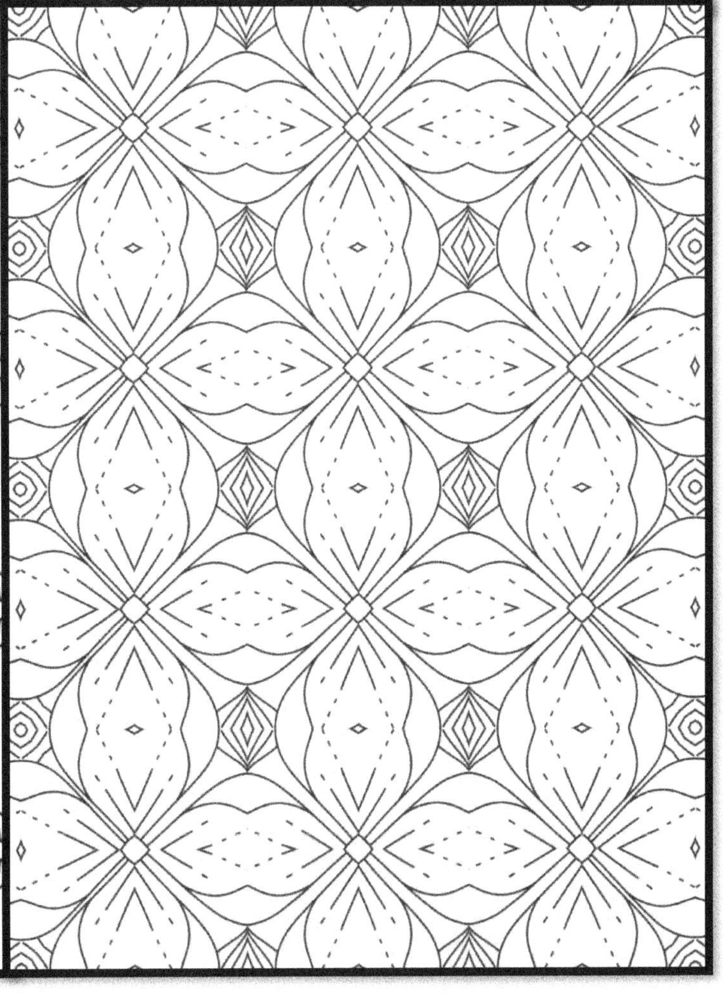

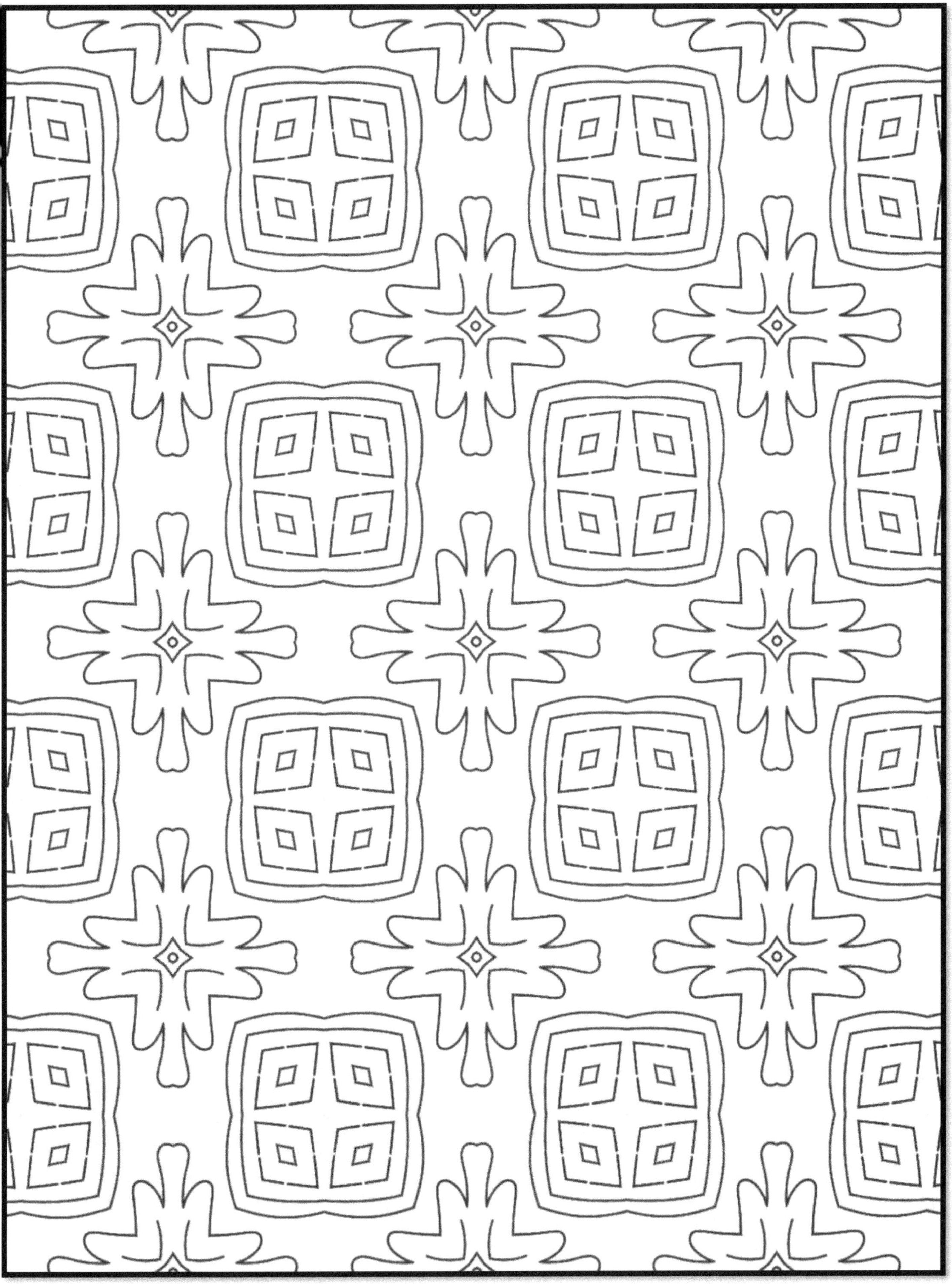

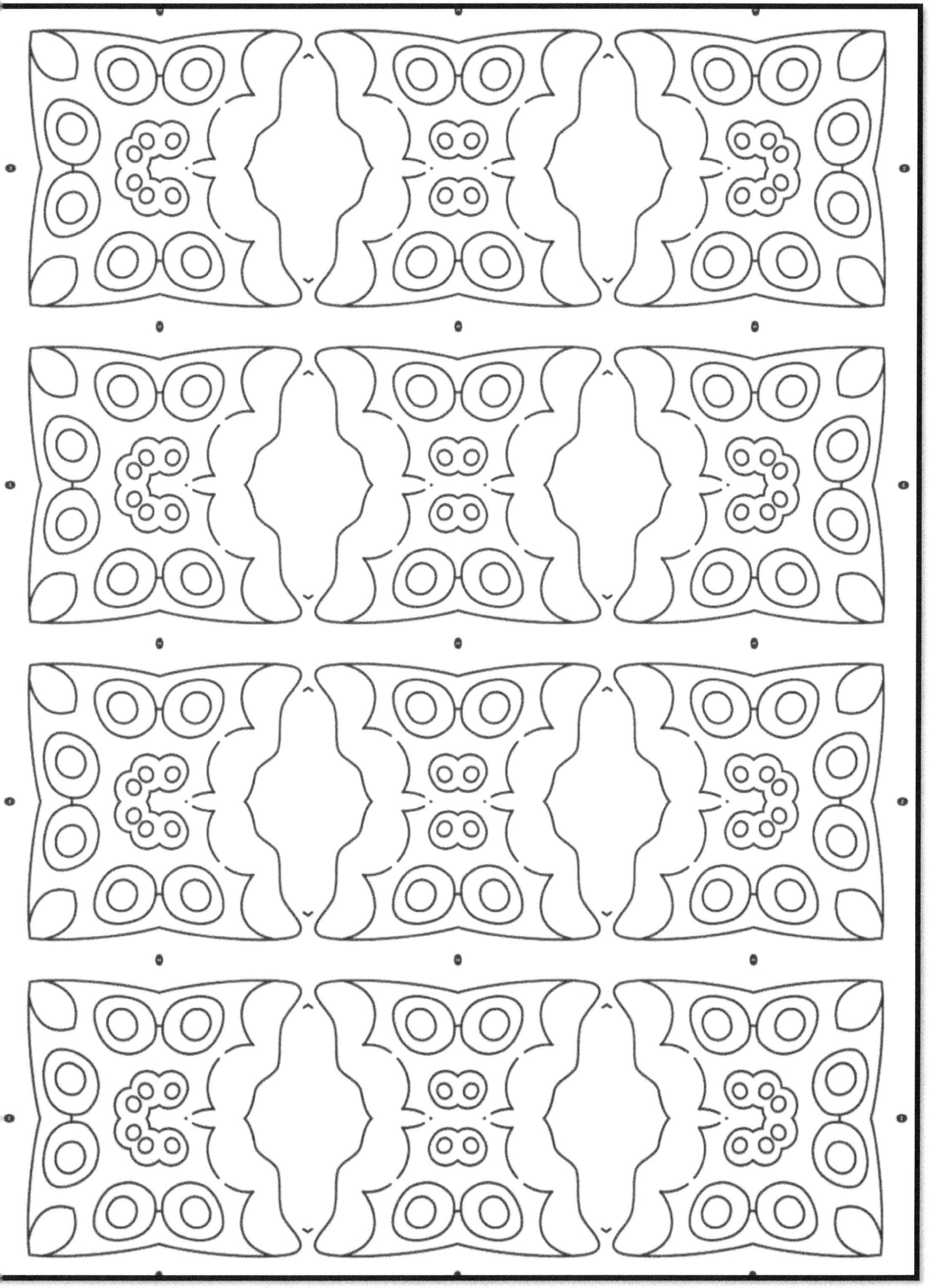

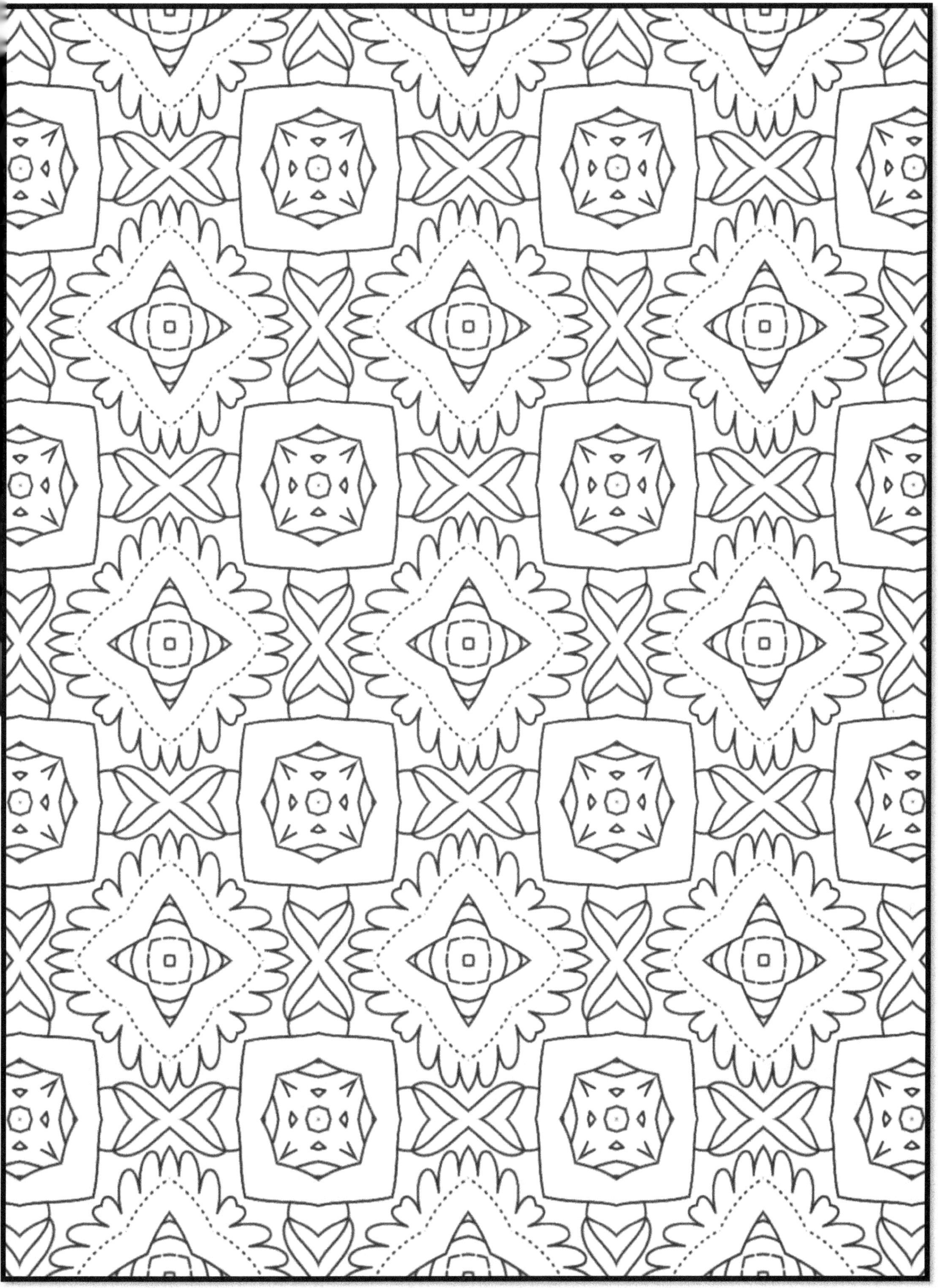

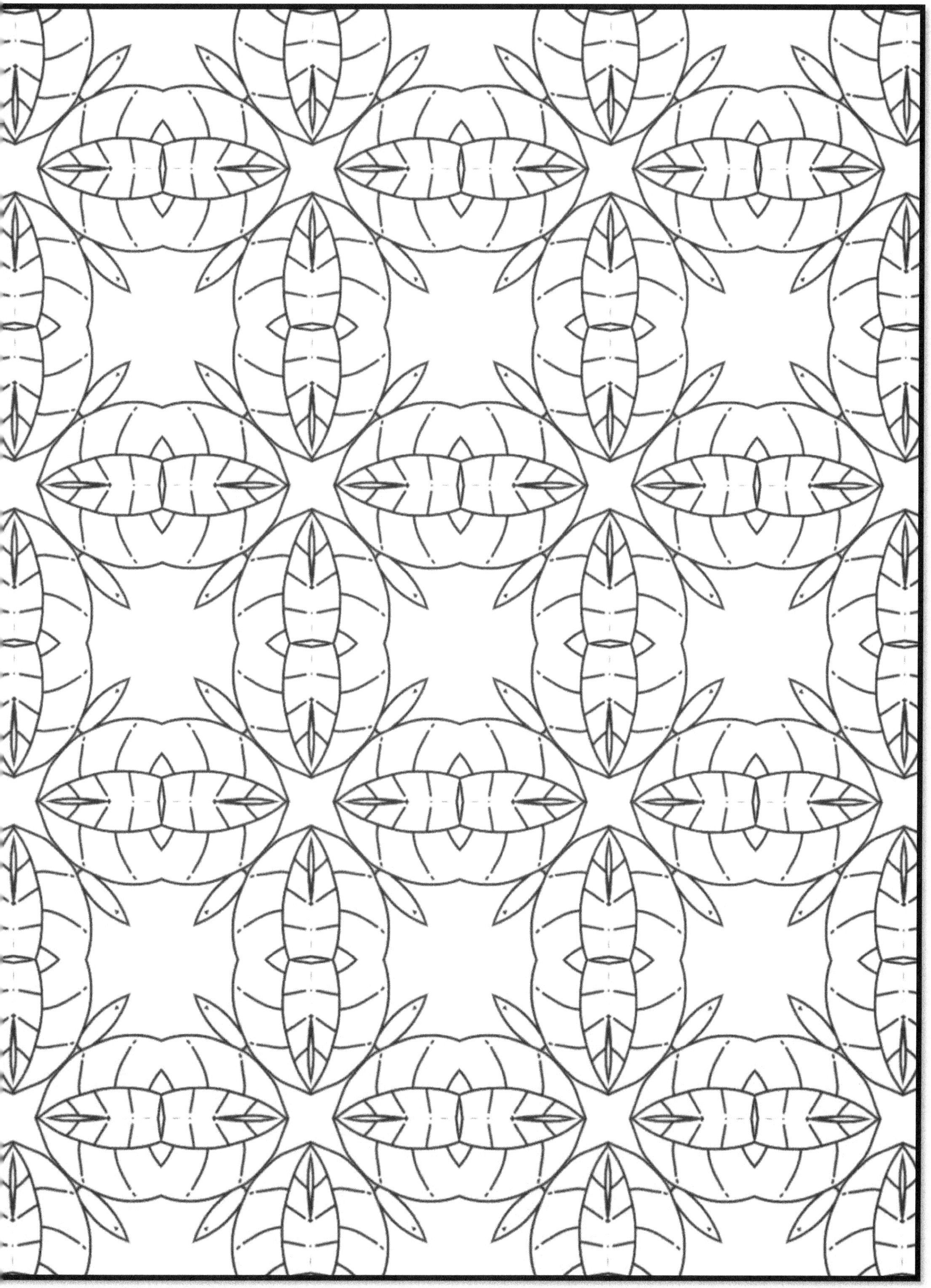

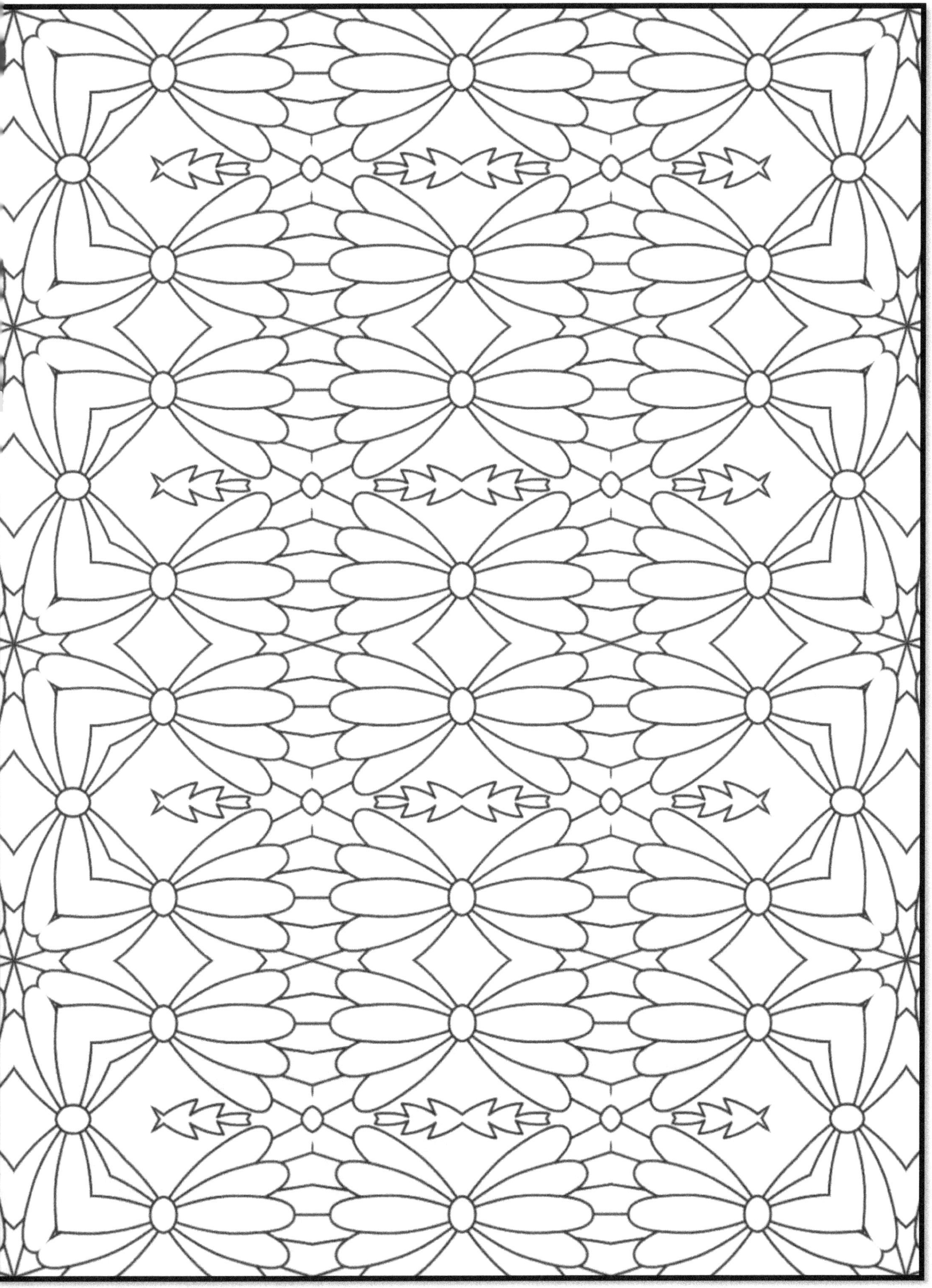

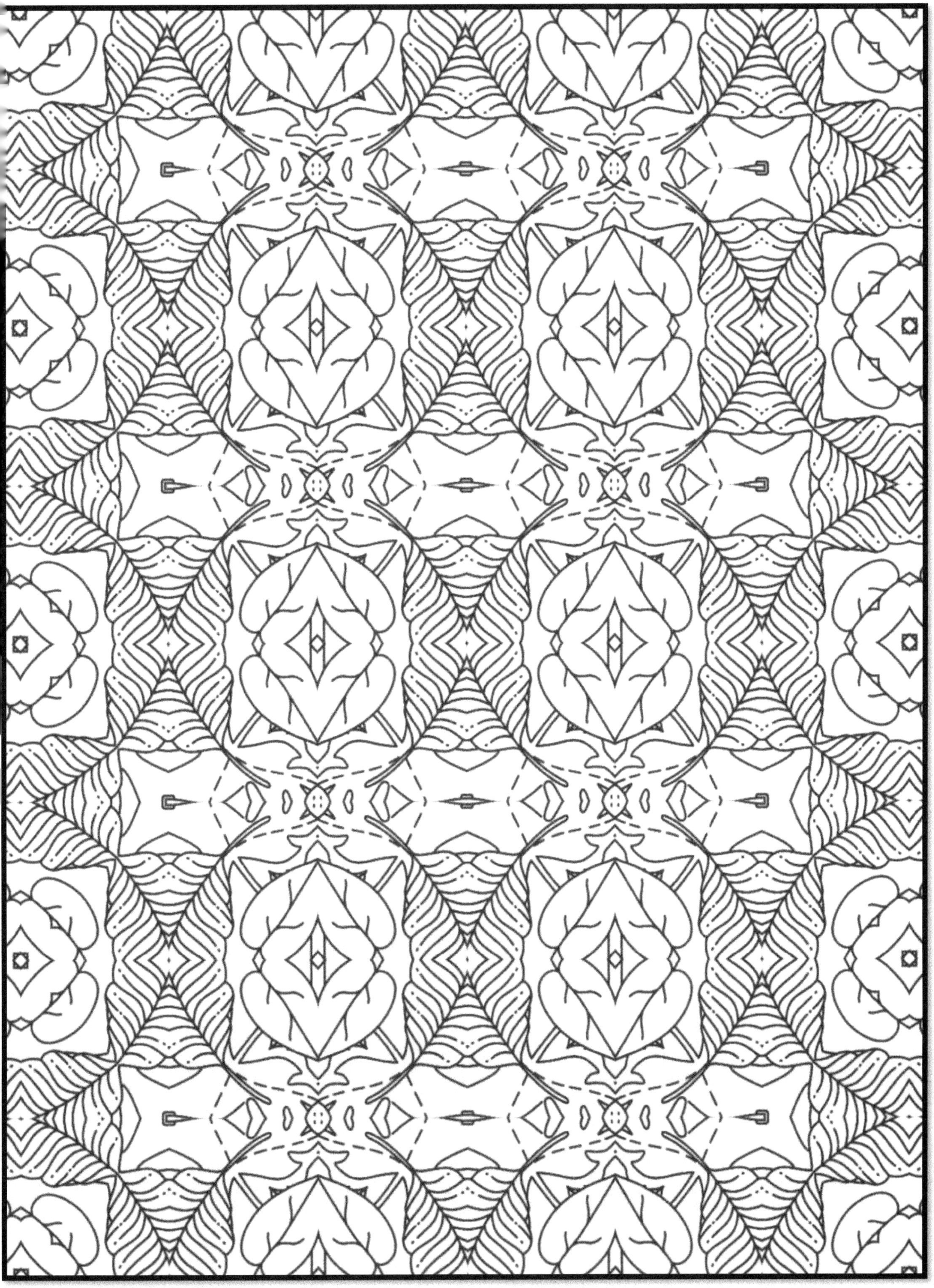

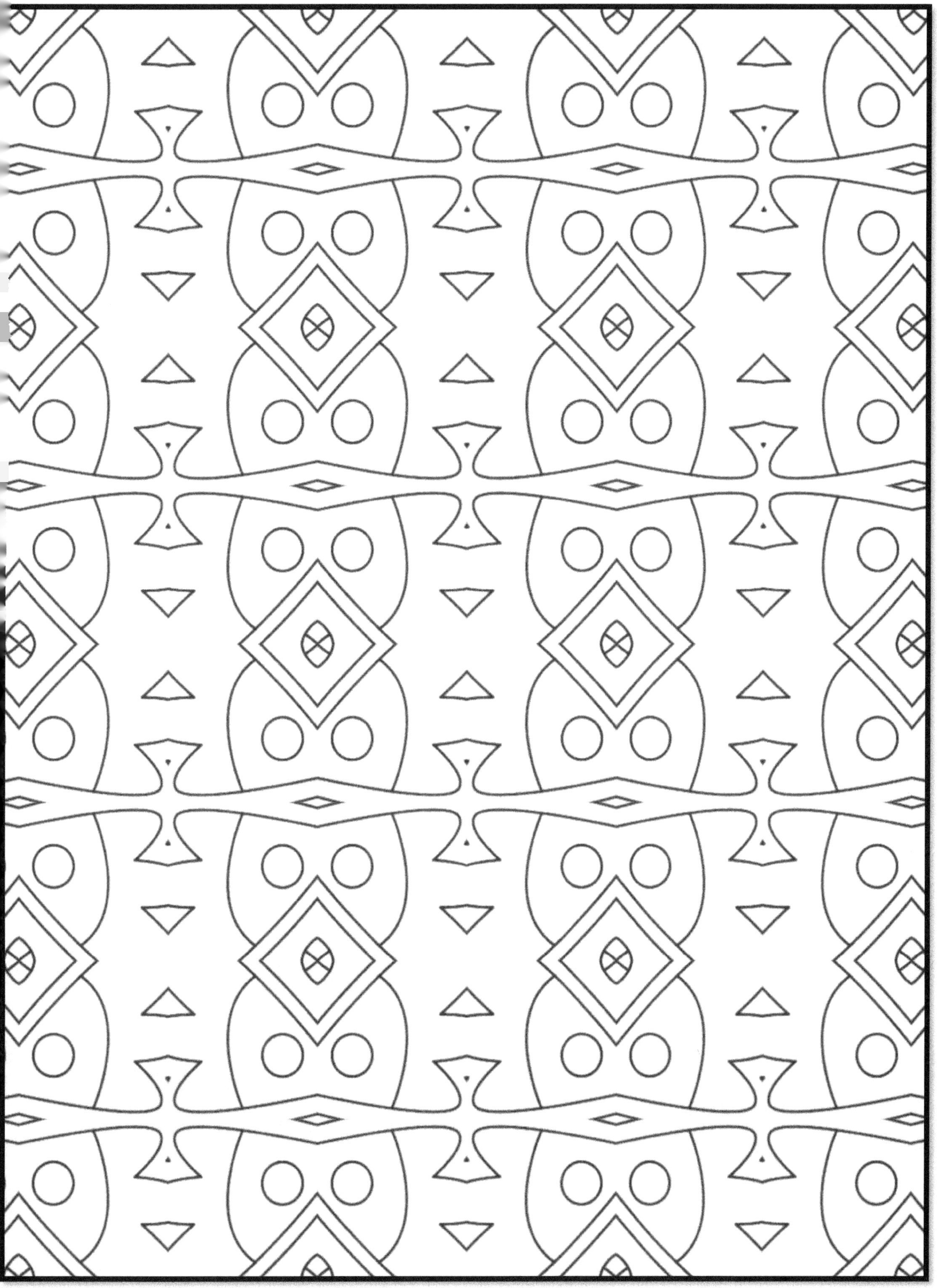

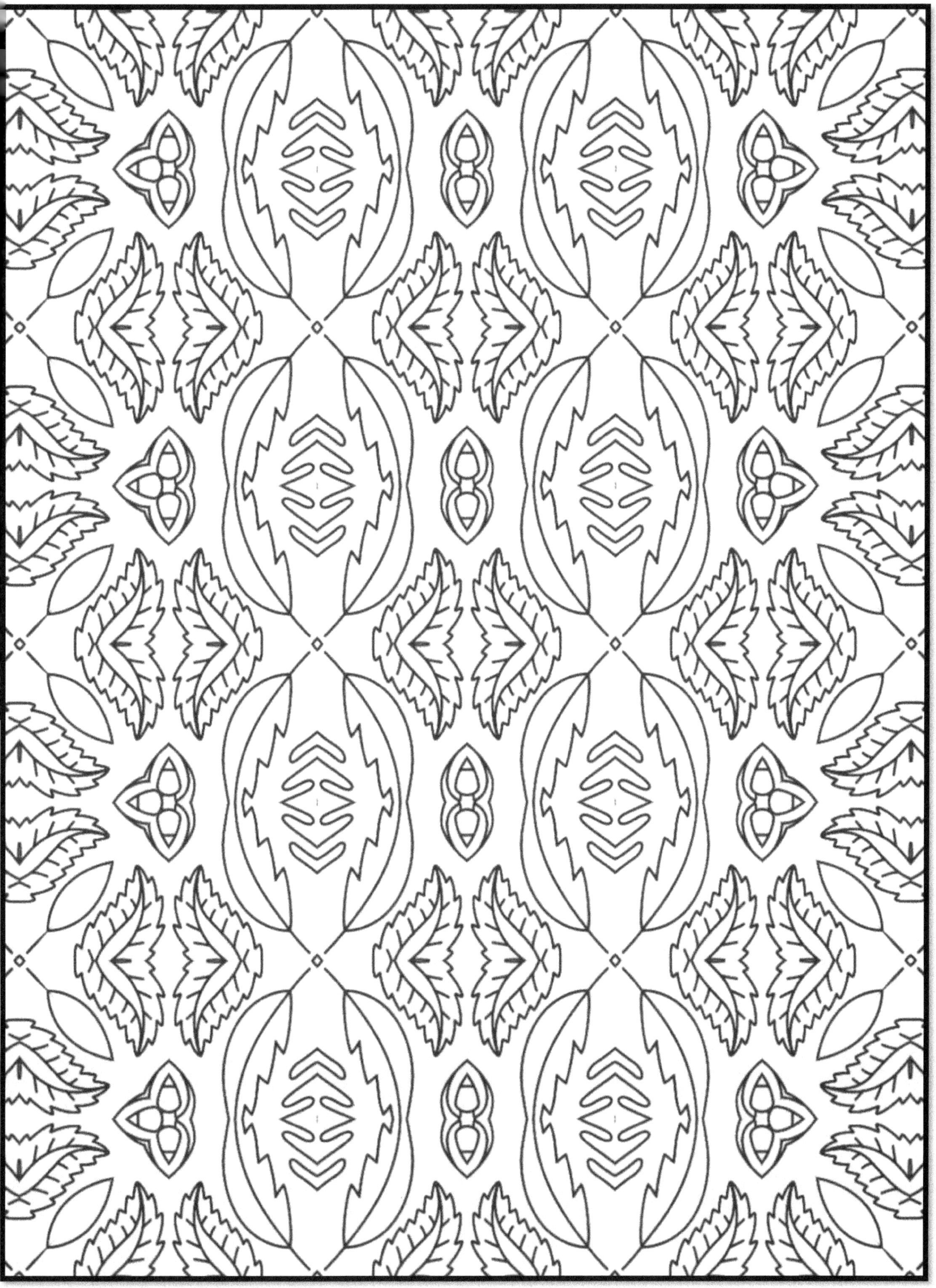

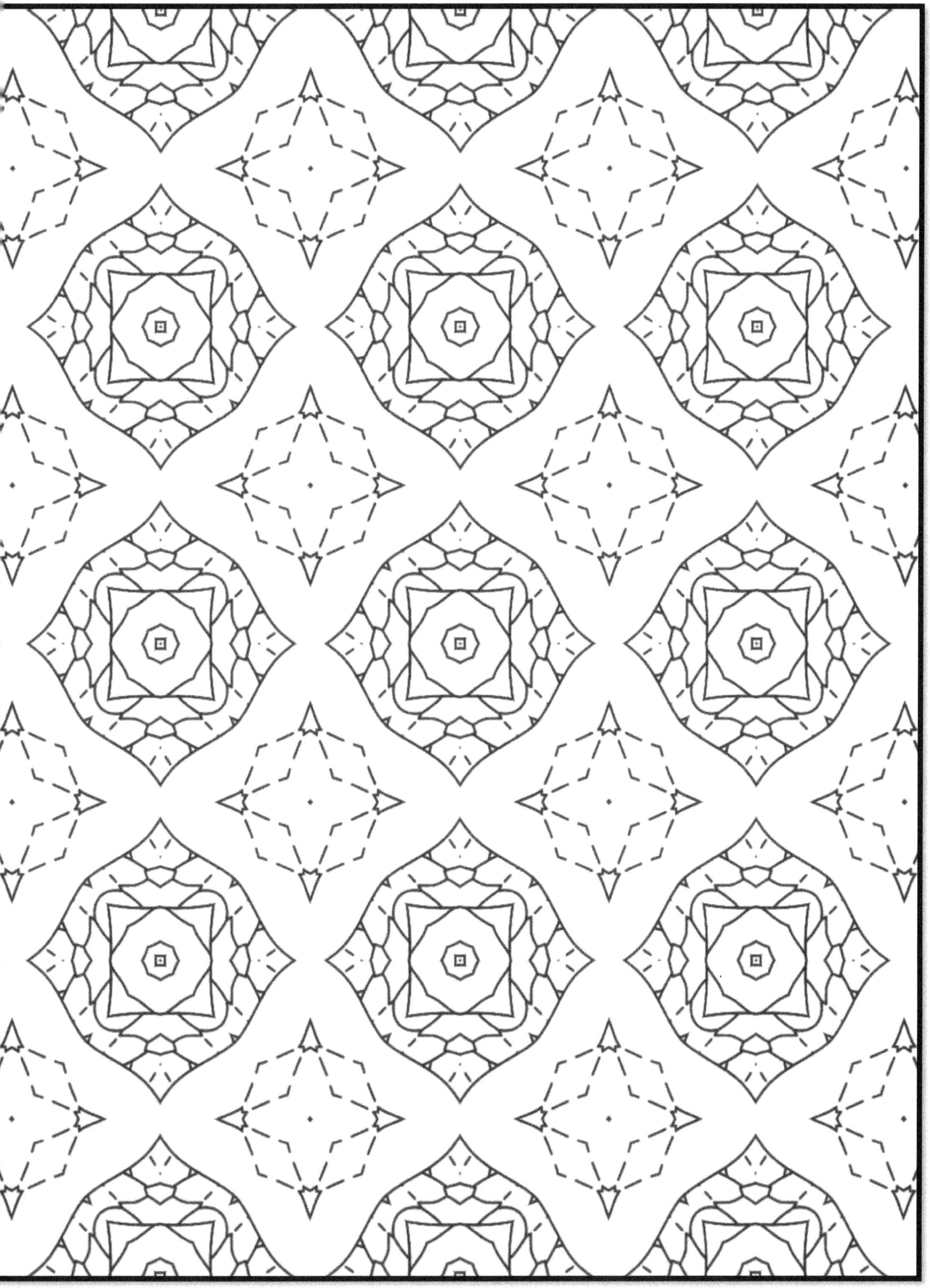

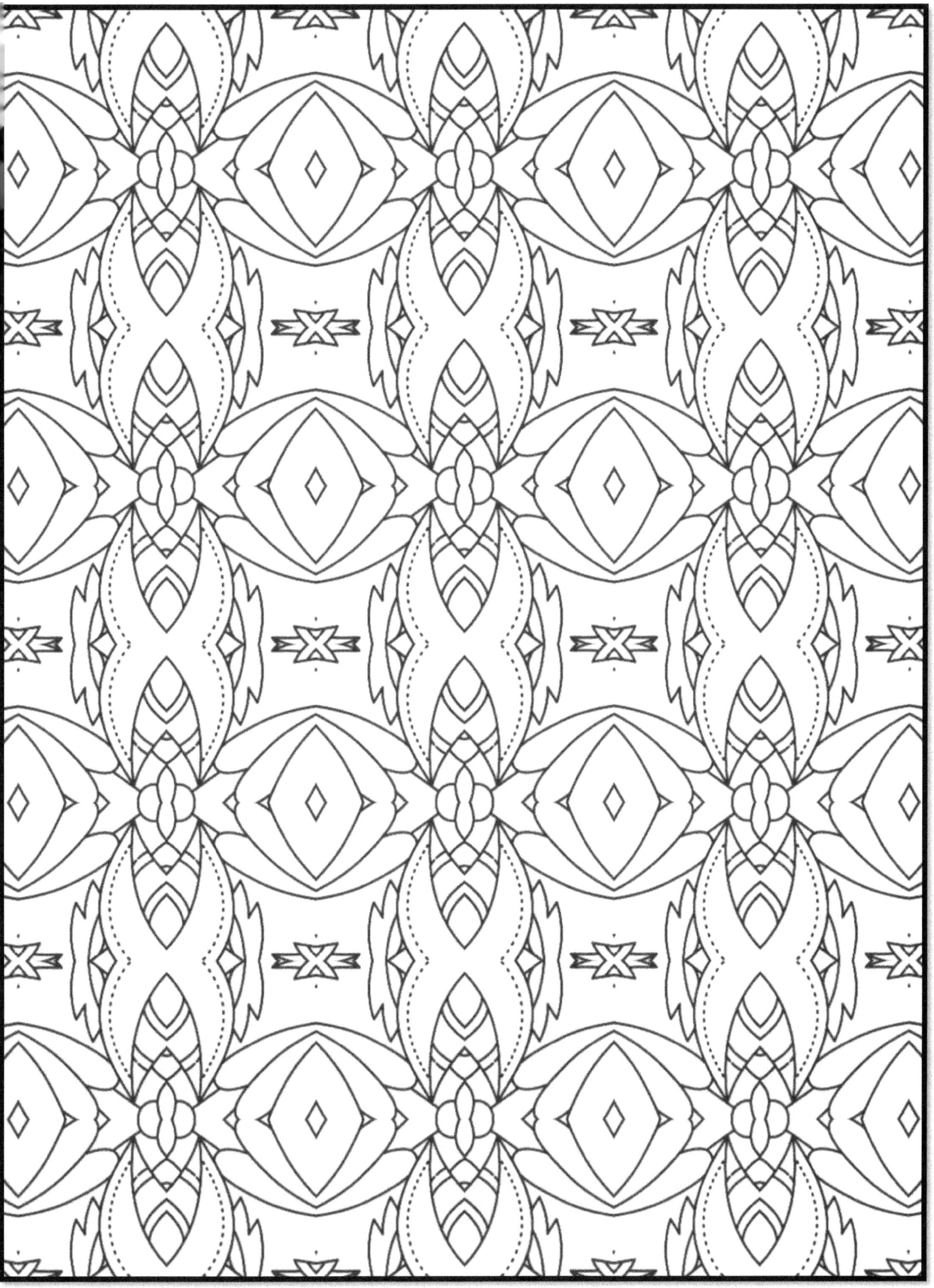

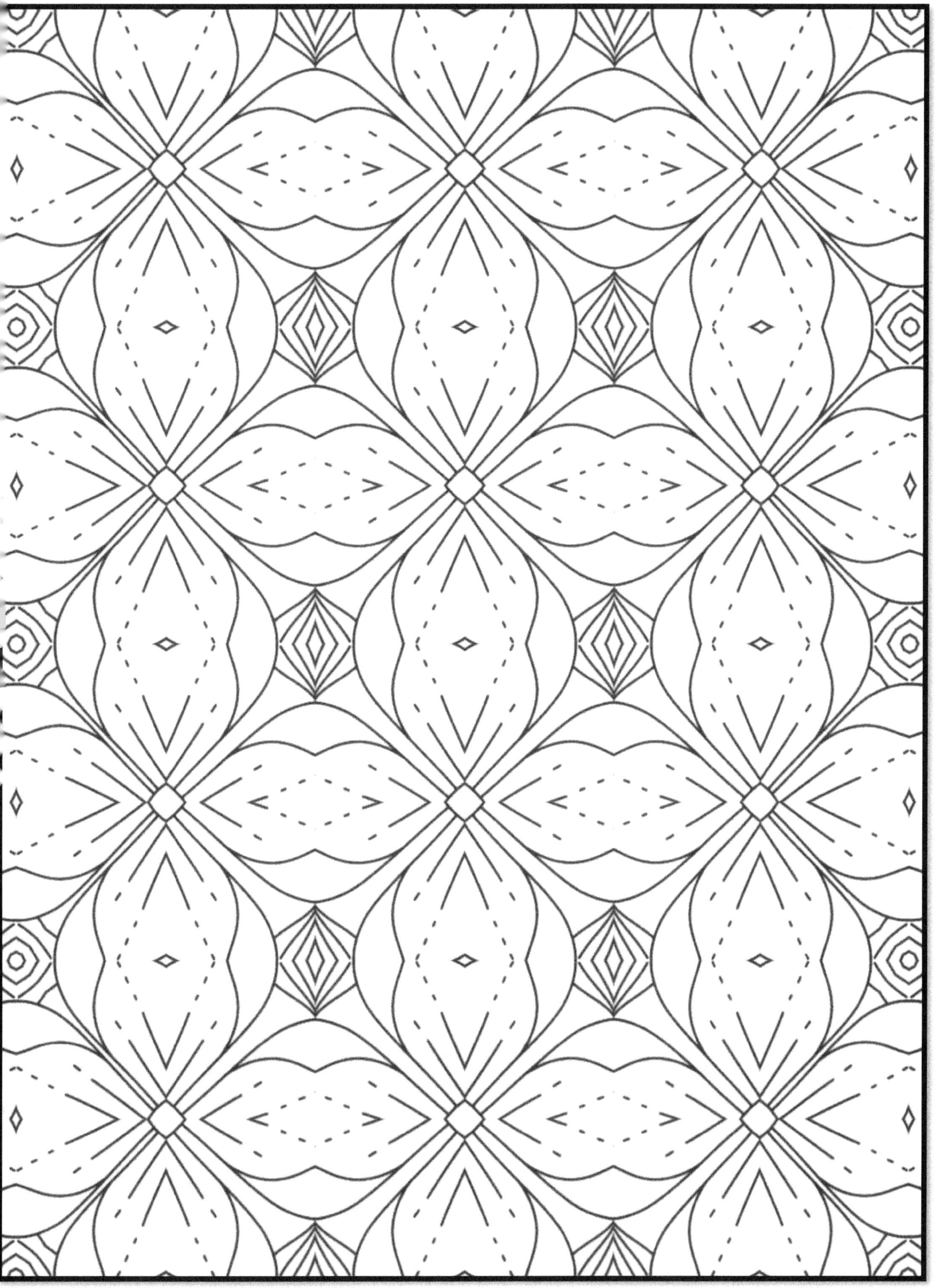

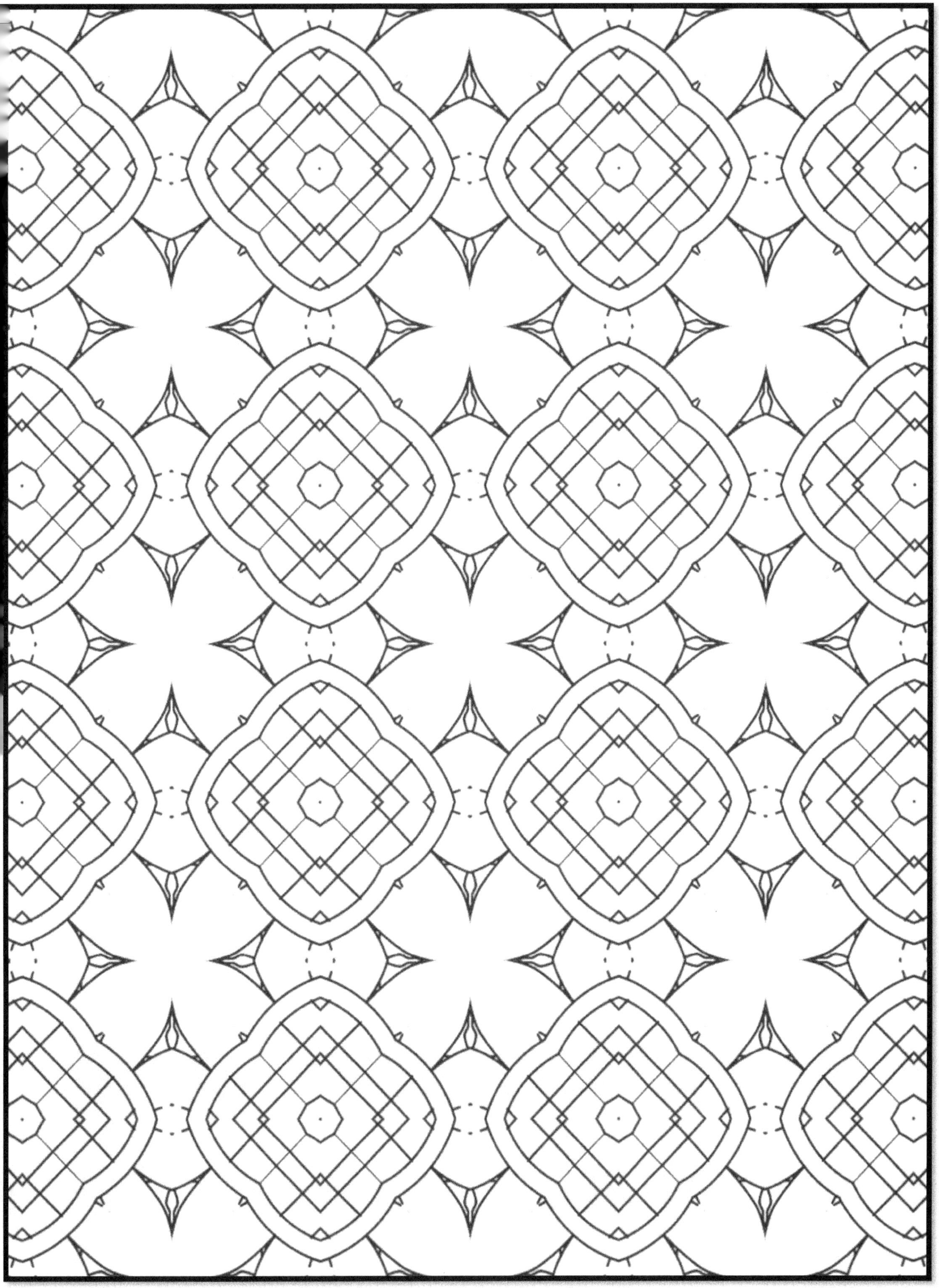

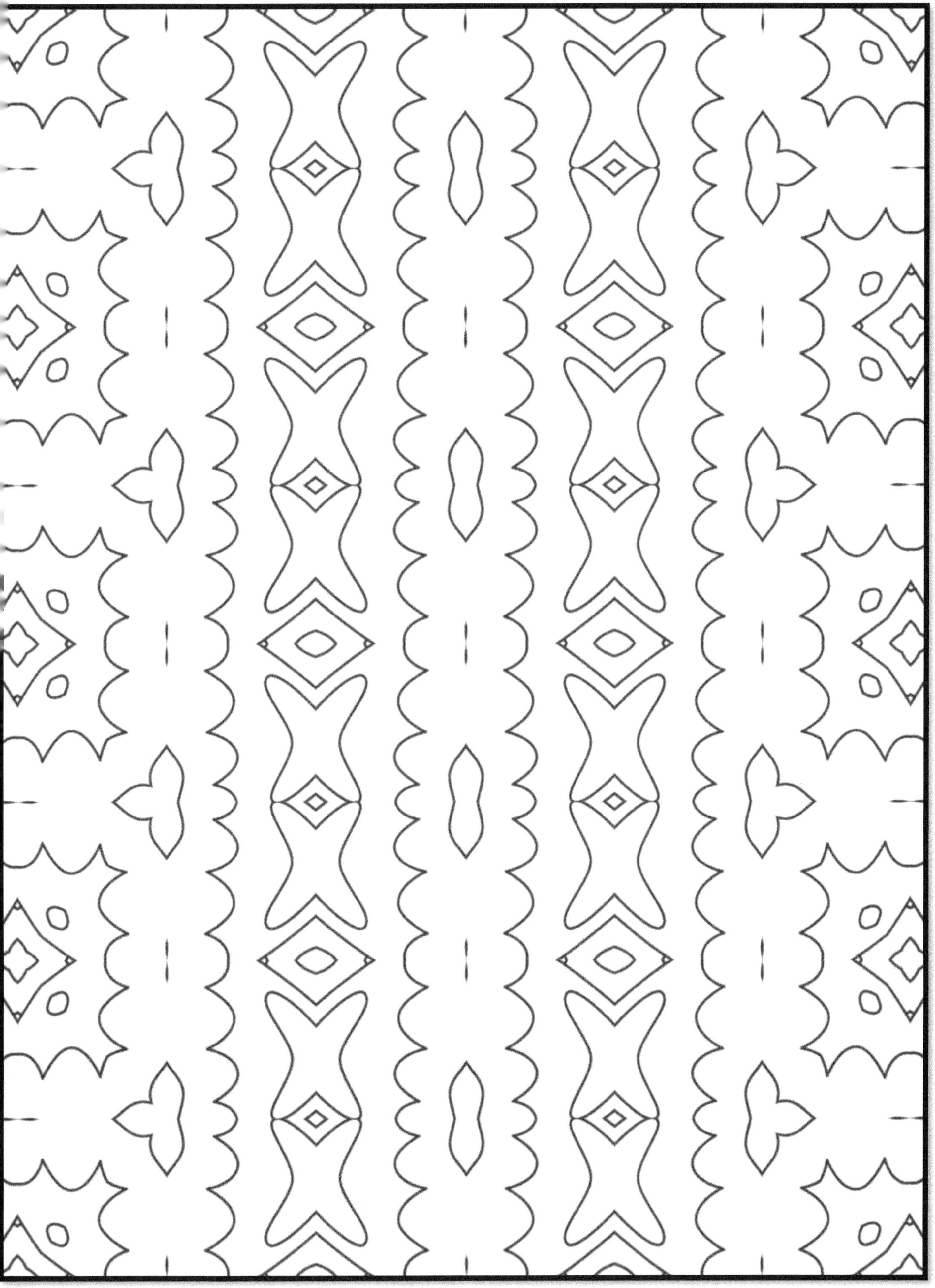

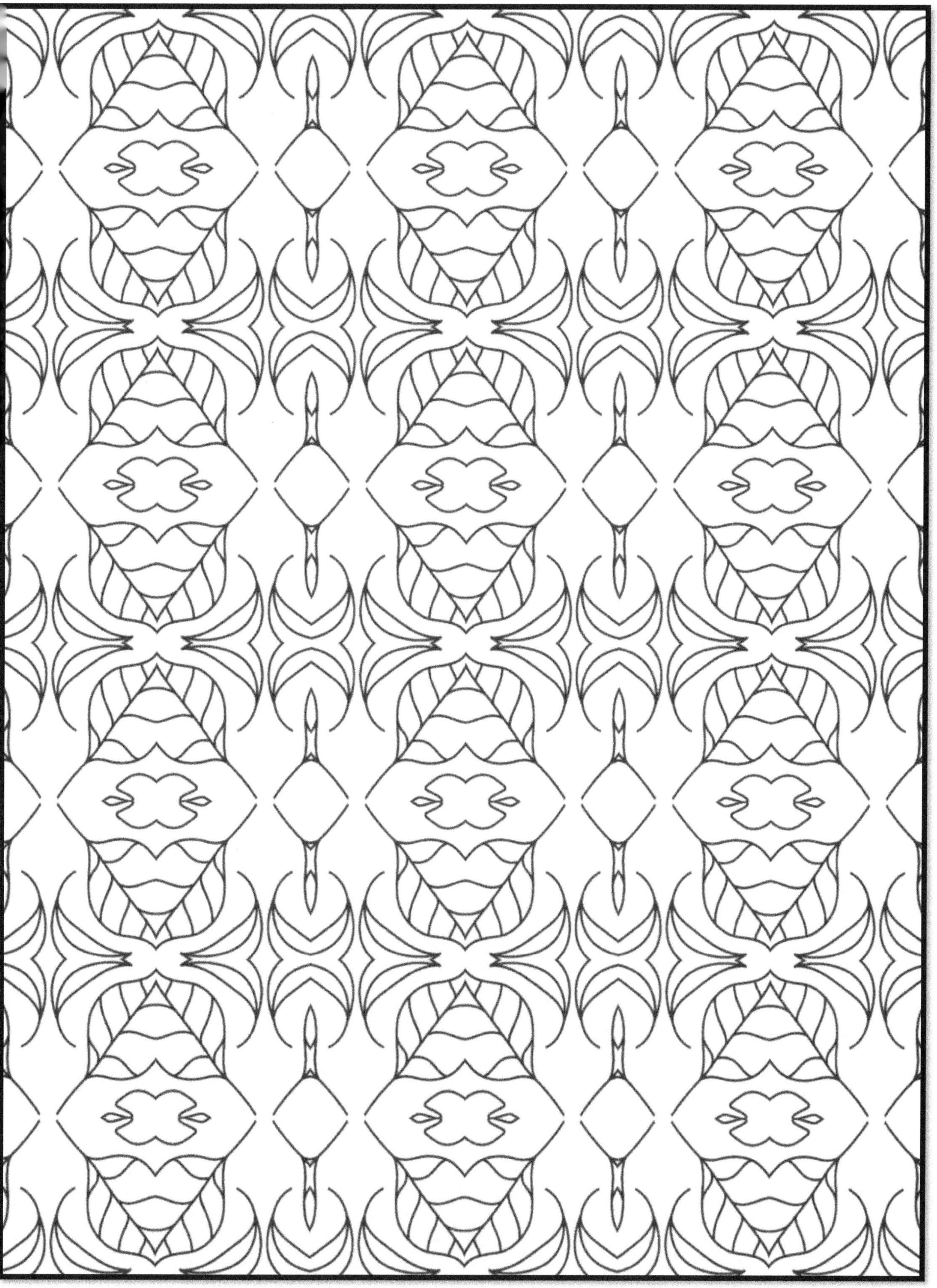

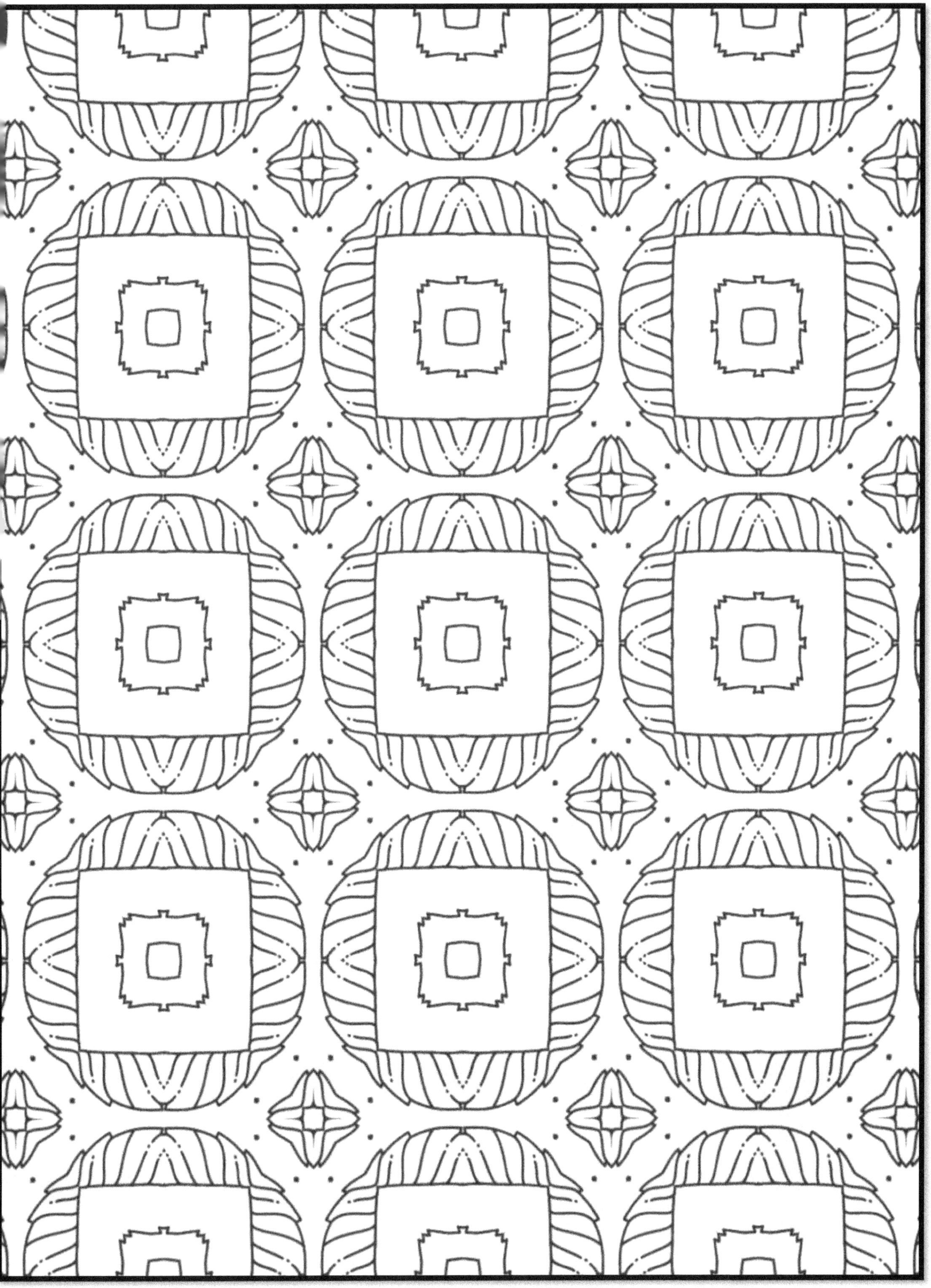

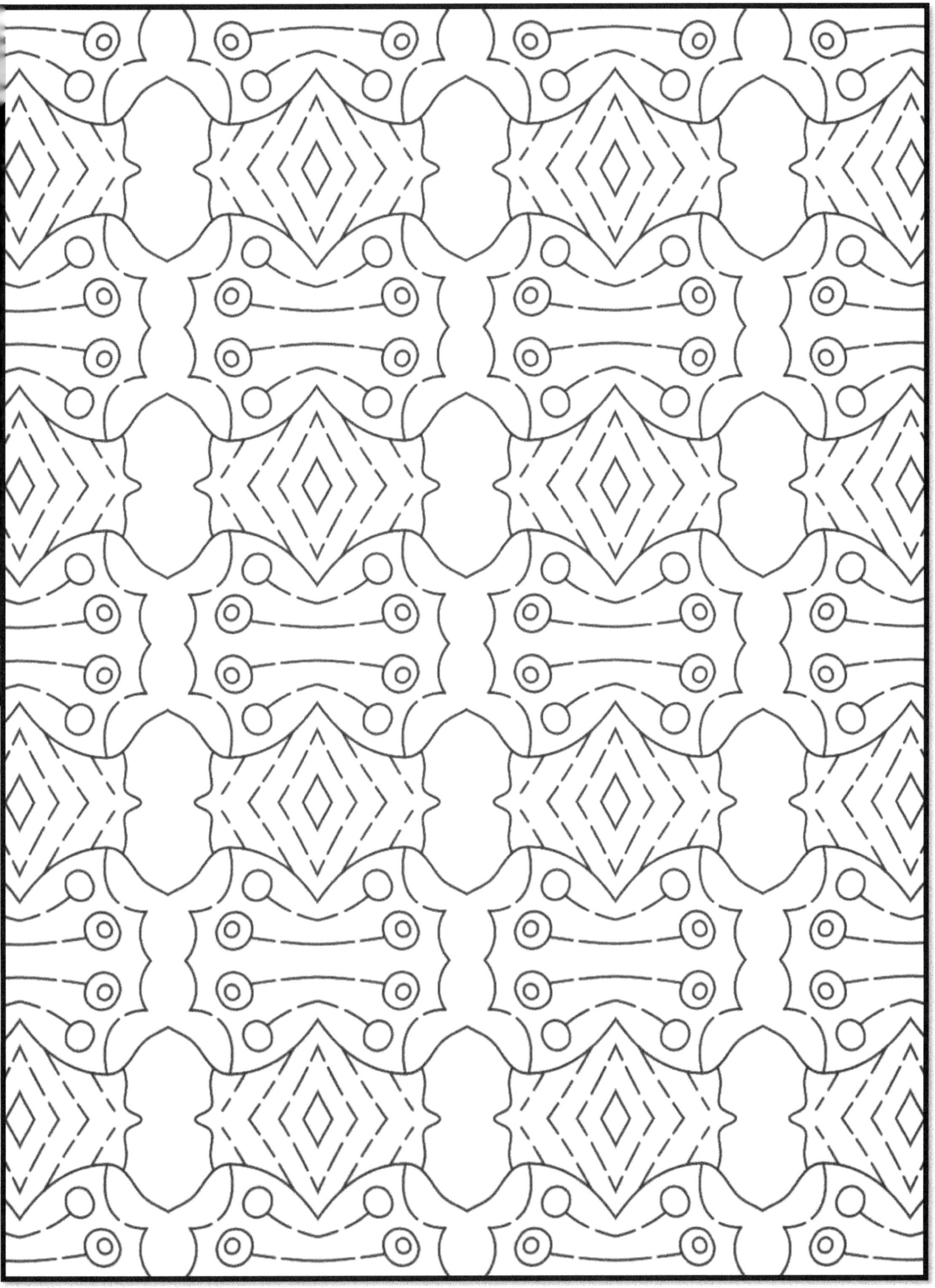

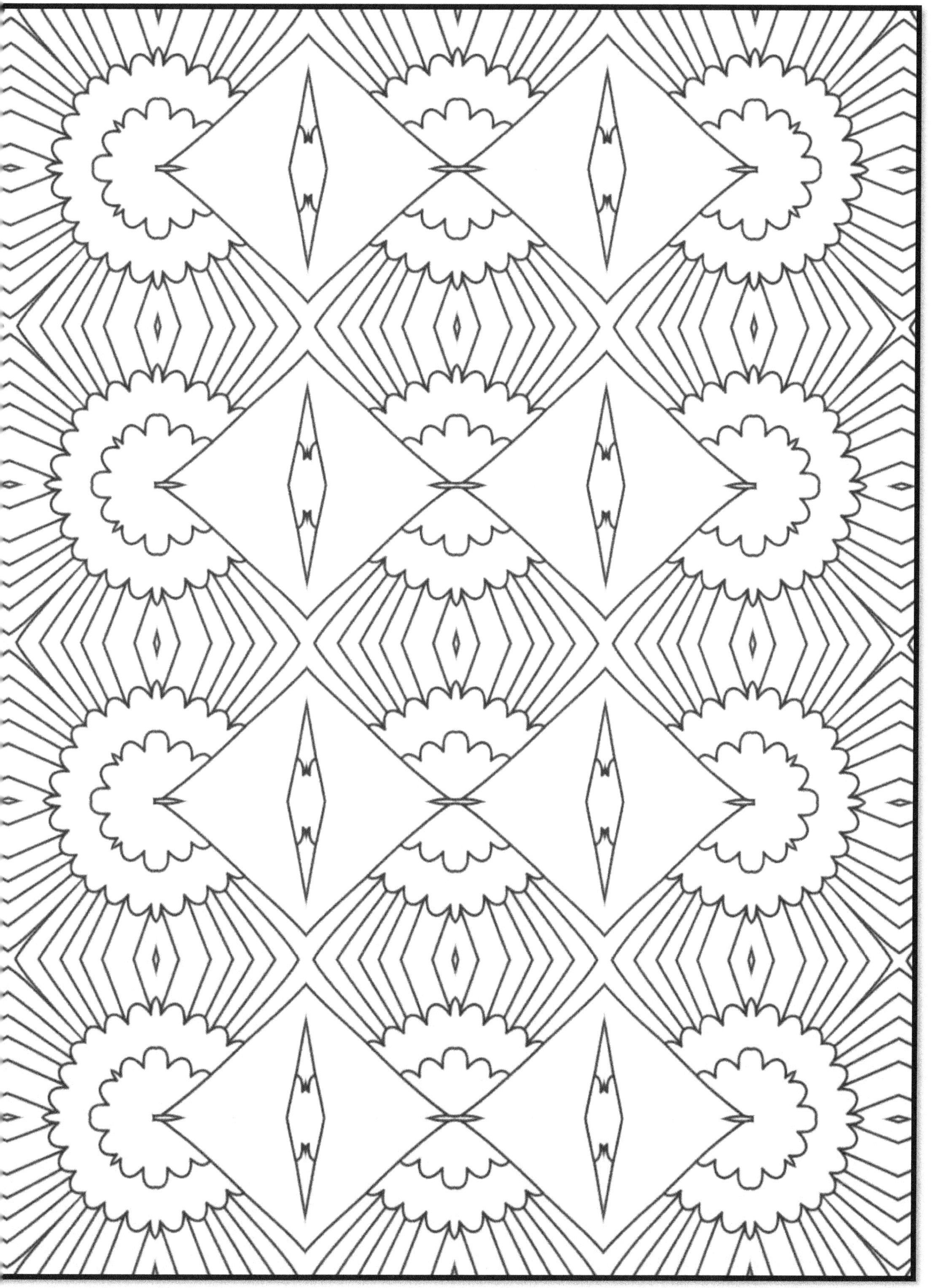

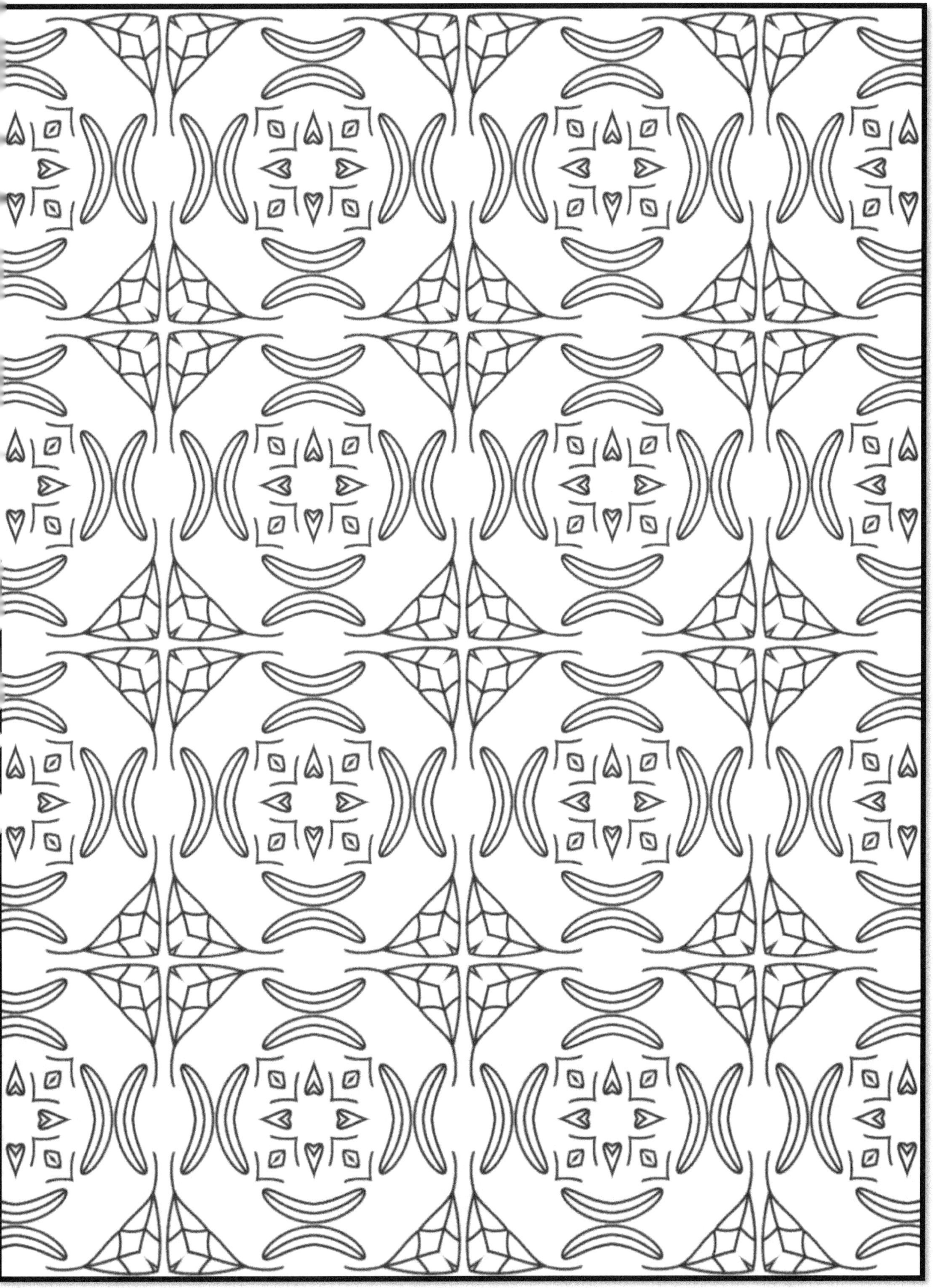

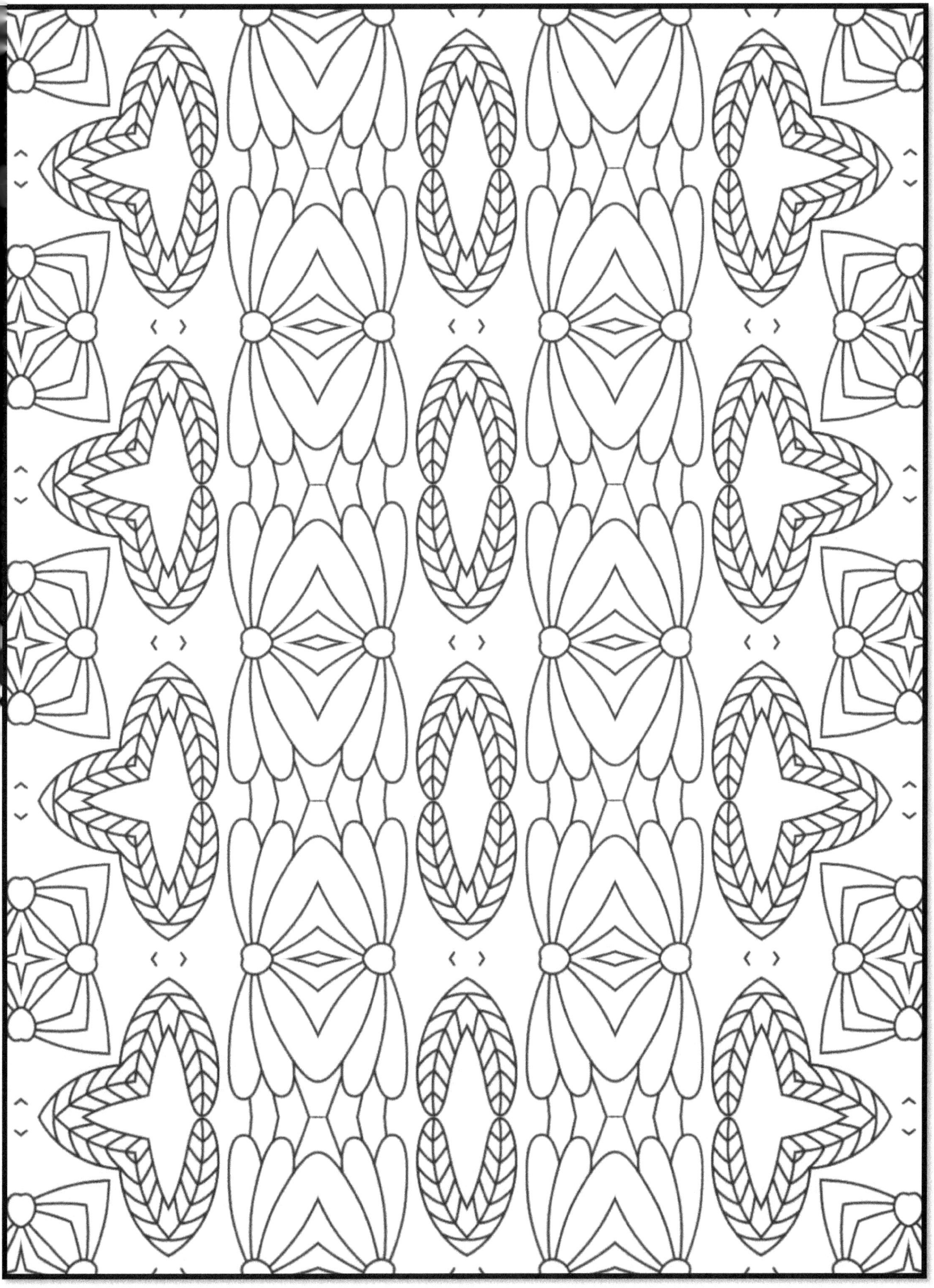

CPSIA information can be obtained
at www.ICGtesting.com
Printed in the USA
LVHW061109110622
721053LV00027B/797

9 798597 700809